SAMPLE AND LOOP

SAMPLE
AND
LOOP

A Simple History of
Singaporeans in America

JEE LEONG KOH

BENCH
PRESS

Published by Bench Press,
an imprint of Gaudy Boy LLC
www.singaporeunbound.org/gaudyboy

Cover design by Flora Chan
Interior design by Jennifer Houle

ISBN 978-1-958652-06-0

For all who live away from where they were born

CONTENTS

SAMPLE AND LOOP

"'Ah then she's not French,' Isabel murmured; and as the opposite supposition had made her romantic it might have seemed that this revelation would have marked a drop. But such was not the fact; rarer even than to be French seemed it to be American on such interesting terms."

—Henry James, *The Portrait of a Lady*

THE HOST

for Paul Rozario-Falcone

(Cornelia Street Café, the Village, New York City, November 5, 2013)

We met for a drink, and one drink turned to two,

two drinks to three, three to a festival

of Singaporean literature in New York,

Bacchanalian altar and Vesta's hearth

for imperious devotees of the arts.

To rally interest, Paul did what he does

so well, hosted a party in his home

in the South Congregational Church, hoisted

in early Romanesque Revival style,

at the intersection of Court and President.

In just ten months, the festival was set.

See! Riding to 92nd Street Y

the donkey or the chariot drawn by pards,

the celebrants of Singaporean stories!

From Texas, whip-smart Wena Poon. From Frisco,

debutante Kirstin Chen. From New York, a tiger

in the kitchen Cheryl Tan and Christine Chia

daughter of the law of second marriages.

From Flushing, Queens, but Singapore Dreaming,

husband and wife Colin Goh and Yen Yen Woo,

killing the readings, with Yakuza Baby.

From Singapore, Alvin Pang, Cyril Wong,

Haresh Sharma with his beautiful Faunus,

Pooja Nansi, Tania De Rozario,

Verena Tay, no strangers to the strange,

bacchantes, priestesses, and oracles,

the soldier-poet, a centaur, Joshua Ip,

and the twice-born, Jason Erik Lundberg,

born in Brooklyn, reborn in Singapore.

Fourteen authors in all, a pop-up store

of Singaporean writing Paul and I

presented for New Yorkers to live in.

Fun while it lasted, but not for long.
The altar and the hearth were missing a note
or two. He sought for it, for them, a while
in choral singing. He still sings, but if
the soul requires its singing-school (and we
had gone to the same schools), the expat body
expects its altar-hearth, the give-and-take
between the body and, no, not the soul,
the building. Not just hermit crab and shell.
Not Brunelleschi and his lofty dome.
Not even the boy and his melanin.

The closest he has come to finding it
was at the new Rizzoli, in NoMad.
Leading a one-day workshop there, he hid
several writing prompts in the bookshelves,
note cards with scalloped edges, looking like
speech bubbles, as dear Al, his husband, said.
A student found a bubble in between
Prefab House and Palladio's Legacy,
and gave voice to the words in cursive script:
Read aloud softly a poem you wrote
as many times as you can bear your voice,
and as you read, live in the space your voice
raises, and write down what it's like to live.
Drippy with a hangover, I read online
Paul's prompt, and in reply wrote this reply:
an open invitation to come in.

THE CERAMICIST

for Hong-Ling Wee

(arr. 1992, New York City)

On a NASA scholarship to map the world,

she walked into a workshop on a whim

to throw a lump of clay on a wheel and feel

a foggy, quiet, pink, revolving world

evolve into an object of the mind

under the body's pressure, slight and sure,

and, afterwards, surrender to the fire,

not that of fire, but that of accident,

for a ceramic rocket fallen back

to earth. And this she did, for many years,

living on little, explaining less, until

she was surrounded by the fuselage.

When the towers gashed vermilion and buckled,

she was alone at home in Union Square.

The noise expanded as it dribbled off

to meet its echo, second detonation

worse than the first report, in summoning

half-buried images of Hiroshima

and Nagasaki. In a foreign mood,

she heard the phone ring, and a female voice,

acclimatized but recognizable

as Singaporean, asked for Wee Hong-Ling.

She never tires of telling this story, how

the Consulate located her and every

Singaporean within an hour of disaster,

when a black hole opened but was avoided

because a star had called, a star called home.

She never tires of telling this story, which
I now tell you in my own fanciful way,
each iteration also explanation,
the how developing into the why,
why her pitchers, bowls, vases levitate.

THE COLUMNIST

for Kopin Tan,

who renounced his Singapore citizenship in October 2018

The questionnaire required him to rank
his top three reasons. Children's education.
Property prices. NS. CPF.
Thinking the answers only acronyms
for the good life defined by Singapore,
he chose to write next to the label *Others.*
He could have said he was the very first
gay Asian columnist for Barron's, and he
threw over the stock market for his novel.
Or, more facetiously, he could have said
he liked Tate's cookies. Or, more tellingly,
the pictures of his SG friends and wives,
but when he posted on his Facebook page
snaps of his husband, deafening silence.
They liked his cheesecake photos well enough.
They did not like the pics of Tom and him.

Before reason number one, before zero,

he was a block away from the World Trade Center,

in Marriott Interviewing some big shot,

when the first tower chased a falling man

down to the ground, and everything the dust

covered turned white. Skittering down, he was

out on the street to cover the event,

following his reporter's nose. Strangers stripped

their dress shirts off for masks and doused them

with bottles given free by hot dog vendors.

The smoldering smell persisted on Wall Street

more than a month later. Once in a while

the subway car would hear a cry, and sob.

He bonded with his city then, I thought,

reading his article, a hymn of love,

a declaration, a new constitution

drawn up and ratified by meeting Tom

in Therapy, the bar and not the shrink,

and marrying in New York's City Hall.

He could have said, gaily, and that is why

I'm turning in my passport and IC,

one long expired, but the other not,

and what he declared would have been a lie.

It would not have taken into account
the sad little bar squatting at the top
of Lucky Plaza, where men fell each night
into their drinks and could no way be dried.
The lonely hours of driving in a shell,
where was no standing up or lying down
but offered escape still, no questions asked
but Whitney's "Don't you wanna dance with me,"
on Nicoll Drive, which ran beside the coast
but wrote and rewrote O, number and letter.
Because of those drowned mouths, he was to write
for his one reason on the questionnaire
the criminalization of homo...
quantified those hours as 377
and graded his own answer with an A.

THE PEDIATRICIAN

for Lakshmi Ganapathi

(WhatsApp video call, October 19, 2019)

The playground, a pin cushion, needles here,
needles there, stuck in her mind but also
the fun of being children among children,
without a care for streaming, only screaming
their hearts and lungs out in mock threat and fear.
The honest threat struck in an HIV hospice
in India, where as a volunteer she heard
a sex worker her age—eighteen—dying
and the steep silence of a stricken mother
whose ten-year-old had died. Their chronicles
made her resolve to work in global health.

Singapore gave next to no room for it
but corridors of senior doctors screaming
at juniors, or else dropping words like acid.
She saw her self changing, her world contracting
to a conveyor belt, another Yeo's
packet drink with a well-wrapped plastic straw.
She wanted more, for herself, for her work,
friends who were less, not more and more, like her.
In Boston, eminent researchers claimed
ignorance unashamedly and sought her views.
Foundations funded her. After five, no calls.
She could spend time on, not just with, her toddler.

And then Trump came along and sent her husband,

an Indian born and raised in rural Texas,

despising the parade of burning crosses,

to bed where he stayed, crying, for two weeks.

The kids in the hospital, many Haitian,

their bodies racked by virulent diseases,

asked her tearfully, will I be sent back?

Her nanny had two children born right here.

The only cure for fear was organizing,

and she did, with the Jamaican Plain Progressives,

to change state policies and affect elections,

regretting all the while that she did not

in Singapore, where fear is virulent.

The vile attacks on Preetipls and Subhas

for rapping against brownface hit home hard.

To organize and work for change is vital.

She's optimistic, her husband far less so.

He knows white nationalism up close,

and as a visitor to Singapore,

brought Kabir to the top of IMM,

where a new playground reached up to the clouds,

a few more touches needed here and there,

plastic wrapping waiting to be unwrapped.

Kabir was screaming merrily on the swing

when a boy—six or seven, Chinese-looking—

cautioned her husband to stop playing there

or else the police would come and catch him.

Heeding the interference of a child,

she walks on hope and fear, on pins and needles.

THE THEATER DIRECTOR

for Mei Ann Teo

(Pershing Square, Grand Central Terminal, Midtown, New York City, June 19, 2019)

Seven years near Boston, from nine to fifteen,

while daddy pondered math education

and wrote his thesis, she was bitch-slapped

right back to Singapore by RGS.

She slipped from top of the class to the arse,

from popular to pariah in one step.

Stupid she was, untalented, and fat.

Much later, Buddhism would teach Mei Ann

the lesson to be drawn from suffering—

the pain dismissed by adults themselves in pain—

to be crushed is a gift and an entrance

to the more horrific pain of others,

Madeline Sayet, for instance, whom Mei Ann

directed at the Globe, whose mother tongue

died facing Shakespeare's, who dared to ask

what if Caliban spoke Mohegan, and

pursued into the plays that New World question.

At VJC, Mei Ann was Caliban
studying Singlish from the secret notes
passed by Christine. The obscenities she learned!
Caliban too she was when she could not
rehearse or perform in her school theatrics
on Saturdays because the day was sacred
to Seventh-day Adventists. At NUS,
she could not take her final Soci exam,
and so she took an F. The way was open
to Pacific Union College, Napa Valley,
where, irony, she let go of her faith.
When the student is ready, the teacher will appear,
and at that time and place, in the guise of
a scholar of five languages, the change
was no decision, but discovery.

Here to refract the white man's grubby view

to cheery faith's vast, rainbow coalition

is now her aim—in dating or directing—

or, rather, to the heart she leads us there,

Mohegan, Maddy translated, for directing,

and when collaboration fails, or falters,

as it will from time to testing time,

to dare to say to all, "Let me ask myself."

THE SCENIC DESIGNER

for Izmir Ickbal

(Patisserie Des Ambassades, Harlem, New York City, March 16, 2019)

What is he doing here? Driving five hours

through whipping snow for a wimpy salary

to teach at a college named after King Alfred.

Stopped on both sides of State Route 86,

cars driven off course by the blinding wind

in the foothills of the Allegheny range.

He shivers. He can feel it in his bones,

the hurricane howling down the corridors.

He used to assess risk, back at the Bank,

of weather, terrorism, protests, strikes,

but how do you assess *you* the assessor?

Grad school was hard but clear. The first two years,

he was tekan by his professors, who

forced him to follow their old formulas.

In the third year, they ordered him to use

his own instincts, which Izmir thought they had

beaten out of him; no, they reemerged

like morning light all over Morningside,

designed to be New York's Acropolis,

their home as the wife goes, in turn, to school.

Impossible in the snowstorm to see
where he is going. He woke up at four,
and the sky is not getting any brighter.
He has a sense, however, he has been
here a long time ago, an ancient sense
of salt, unfurling sails, fortunate soil.
Coming of age in Singapore, he found
his place not with the Malay boys—he tried—
but the Eurasian kids. His Chinese father
grew up living with Indian foster parents.
(Izmir can make an excellent biryani.)
His mother's Malay father broke the rules
and hearts by marrying a Portuguese,
an enemy, if history is to be believed;
if love, an archangelic touring singer
who took the name of Lena Abdullah.
"Don't You Remember," Adele in his car
sang on his way to work, past HarbourFront,
when he accepted his acceptance—Yale!—
and cried, not least for Zizi's happiness,
Zizi who woke him before the sun was up
in early April, Zini still asleep,
and shouted, "Baby, baby, you got in!"

THE CONDUCTOR

for Phillip Cheah,

born in Louisiana, 1978

He never saw her without makeup on,
his pretty mom who had a different hairdo
in every photograph she left behind.
Stylish as she, the son never left home
without his Brylcreem helmet and his suit,
well favored by the flower of a tie,
Anita Mui from her radio in his ears.
A misfit with his peers, he gravitated
to teachers, who in every year made him
a monitor in Rosyth and RI.
The love of music begun at puberty,
after some years of banging ivories
when he was taught composers and their times,
and music gathered faces and debates,
closeted Phillip further—Tchaikovsky!—
in Yamaha's CD library near Balestier.
The blissful hours lost in listening,

listening, listening, and listening.

His father, the geophysics engineer,

wanted to give his draftee son a choice:

Go Singaporean/Stay American.

Music, like his mom, did not give him one.

No conducting school to go to here,

everyone played the piano or violin,

and to conduct was what he was to do.

At nineteen, the boy flew to Bloomington,

Indiana, to take up his birthright,

failure propelling him with fearful fumes,

first in the country of Bernstein, and then

his city, charging hard from gig to gig,

then to direct the Central City Chorus

while he accompanied New York's elite

in tuning up their vocals for the world,

where we met, when somebody (was it Karyn?)

told him, funny coincidence, there was

another Singaporean in the school.

As the intent for tempo clarified
from Beethoven onwards, the instrument
changing from heartbeat to the metronome,
so we discovered the disparate ways
by which we know the same Alvin Tan,
teacher to you and paragon to me.
What we talk about when we talk about
mothers is meter, the stress *on* the beat,
the knuckles, violent roses, that you raise
in concert with your slim baton, and that
she caned to make you learn to tell the time.

THE DAUGHTER

for Marguerita Choy

(Barawine, Harlem, New York City, December 10, 2018)

They had always had animals at home,

welcoming every stray, kittens and pups,

into the house on Jalan Emas Urai,

the kinder of the neighbors named The Shelter.

Better god's creatures than the devil's beasts.

Her father grew up in occupied Ipoh

and, to help his family, sold vegetables

under the noses of the Japanese.

Her mother was an Austrian who did not

care for the Germans. The Americans

neither when their planes strafed a passenger train.

They met in London, after World War II,

he a law student and she an au pair,

and made a family home of Singapore.

Now they live in the city of Dundee,
where she and her sister had gone to school,
and where the older stayed to doctor fate
and bring up her own alien family.
A link, a leash, tenuous and Scottish.
Her mother now alone in a nursing home,
a fact her father forgets when he wanders
beyond the confines of his house to search
for missing animals. The year's been hard,
hardly a golden year. Right in New York,
Reuters is cutting staff to the bone.
Her cat has sprung a fang, and it looks bad.
This Christmas, she will leave with Clay and Mag
the ailing pet and with the ailing parents
spend what little time she has to spare
from her preoccupation with Lafayette.

THE ANALYST

for KK

(Talad Wat, Hell's Kitchen, New York City, November 12, 2019)

A canteen stallholder, his mother traded
in futures when she begged the principal
to admit, first, her daughter, then, her son
into Nanyang Primary—when he gets old,
he'll also need two chopsticks to eat with—
and father, a cab driver, had a weak heart.
Off the boy sped on the course, Chinese High,
Hwa Chong JC—no need for luck, he scoffed—
Imperial College on a scholarship.
He was too smart for engineering work
and corporate bullshit, so he broke his bond,
borrowing from his parents, still the traders,
and studied fluid dynamics at UIUC.
The multiple nights nagging at a question
with not a clue how to approach it: he
saw in his peers the ease he once possessed;
the face of his dead father in his dreams

he saw, or else while driving down Main Street.
Time to cut his losses. Wall Street called.
Opting for Lehman Brothers (Barclays now)
over Constellation Energy,
he prices futures, the more opaque products.
To model human behavior requires a lot
of right assumptions, but it can be done.
The pay is good, some of the work engrossing.
Of course, there are trade-offs, for individuals
as for nations: a software that is quick
will not be accurate. For an instance,
his girl is growing up American.

Not that he feels so much for Singapore,

but every night he reads her, without fail,

a classic Chinese poem to teach the language—

when you left home, you were a pint-sized kid,

when you come home, your hair has grown rice-white,

in my own quick and dirty rendering—

so that his daughter can say to his mom

in tones free of error, without a broker,

ni chi bao le ma, at the very least.

THE FATHER

for W.

(Chengdu House, Chelsea, New York, City, March 6, 2019)

What was compassion he learned when he helped
his older son fill out his college forms.
He wasn't so neglected his abuela
had to report to Children's Services.
He didn't grow up in a foster home.
He hadn't, every season, to meet strangers
before he graduated out the system,
to play basketball to make them like him,
afraid the whole time they would make him choose
between a real home and his younger brother,
or su hermano would choose home over him.
What would Admissions think of A's expulsion
from school for selling his classmates his meds?
What of the second time he had to leave,
this time from boarding school, in the same year
as Trump's election? Rapists, criminals,
the president labeled all immigrants.

Not long ago the same slander applied
to men who lived with men and wanted sons.
In Singapore, the technocrat's wet dream,
he chose and was, it seemed, chosen by merit.
Coming from No-Name School to RJC,
he thought the students smug. Instead of joining
Humanities, he chose the Arts stream to root
for local faculty. Instead of the Ivies,
he studied fashion at Parsons. Instead of
the Chelsea boy, he dated older men,
much older men, with stories of surviving
conversion therapy, gay bashing, AIDS,
heroic stories of protest and care.
He met his husband on Craigslist. He googled
the value of his home to judge it safe,
as he had always done. He didn't know
about the shootings in the neighborhood.
So much for Singapore-style planning! How
could he imagine, in one year, he would
marry in February, graduate in May,
and in June have the boys move in with them?

He had always been good at being trained,
and the adoption training was not hard,
good at filling out forms, following rules,
at cost-and-benefit analysis,
but he had to be taught again and again,
by Christmas cacti as well as the boys,
their shooting, flourishing, yet homely needs
informing his attention, the feeling of
fear inalienable from fatherhood.

THE AUTHOR

for Kevin Kwan,

who moved to Houston, Texas, at the age of eleven

No fences. Cool. No sentry boxes. Cool,
the driveway stripes, the handkerchief-neat lawns,
like in the movies, *Home Alone*, or something.
He was not so hot about no maids. Lunch box
he had to pack himself and find his way
not only to but through Clear Lake High School,
the normal life his father engineered,
far away from hereditary privilege.

Who would anticipate the terminus,
the cancer in the family that struck
by lottery and made him drop New York
for an uncertain term by his father's bed?
There they turned over still-bright memories
of Singapore, the gate that always squeaked,
the taste of Newton wanton mee, the click
of mahjong tiles, the garden birthday parties,
and shared a joke or else a thought, a word
or three, like crazy rich Asians. And yet
another privilege—the clean, white pillow
grew hot under father, and he flipped it
for a cool offertory to the head.
I know he did. Last year I did the same.

THE CHRISTIAN

for Caleb Goh,

married in San Diego, California, in December, 2017

Cries from Within, his father's text on sex-
change surgery, a sympathetic text,
the title hints, titled his graduate thesis
on carving out a Singaporean voice
in musical theater, the all-American art.
He had been writing it all of his life,
beginning with a grandfather who toured
Asia with Billy Graham as translator,
and parents who sacrificed their twenties
on campuses crusading hard for Christ.
In DC, where they lived for mother's studies,
the boy was bullied over his weird lunch,
homemade fried rice in a fat thermos flask,
and Evelyn's pink hair band he tried and broke.

The bullying kept up in Singapore—
eh you talk so angmo pai—the trying too,
jerking off a man at Kallang Theatre
after Ken Hill's *Phantom*, his mom going
catchily—you pang sai is it take so long.
Another matriarch would go on to say,
in his first role, in the first English soap,
I'll crush you like a cockroach! No help needed
in the drugs, drinking, and sex spree that followed,
even as his fame grew with his drag turn
in *Forever Fever*, which his father watched three times,
and as the nerd in *Teenage Textbook*, until
on a bad trip he tried to drown himself,
as if it was possible, in a toilet bowl.
He stopped himself in his tracks and backtracked.

Those cries subsided, and yet others rose
when Caleb flew to San Diego State.
On stage, as on the site Adam4Adam:
No Asians, please. Sorry! was what he heard,
even from other Asians, so he ate
pizzas and burgers only, eschewing Asia,
and did not go home for three years. So hard
to pass for white, it did not last. What changed him?
Catching the teaching bug and the surprise
discovery that he was good at teaching,
so good they named a dance award after him,
although he was not dead, rich, or alum.
Every year, still, the top dance student wins
the Caleb Goh Dance Award at La Jolla.

Imagine his disgust, back at LASALLE

in Singapore: no Singaporeans, please,

was what he heard, even from Singaporeans,

we think white people are better, white people

who think it cool to set *Cabaret* in Bugis,

as if removing drag queens is the same

as killing Jews; who dress Red Riding Hood

in kimono and Jack of the Beanstalk

in a rice farmer's hat. And they were not

even Americans, they were Australians!

And then it happened, in a big revival
of Alfian's *Asian Boys*, which I caught, not
having seen the original, Caleb stared
into the stands and saw, o god, his future
husband, who had a boyish crush on him
since *Textbook*. Bitten but not shy, he was ready
to move back home, but Dickson wished to see
America, and so they did, together,
the treasure island of ten thousand voices,
the foghorns, the debates on campuses,
the quiet streets, the carousel, the music
of freedom born again in the USA.
They could live here. They could. They could walk down
the aisle in Sandi's Presidio Park,
even with Caleb's father praying hard
in a hotel room next door to the Day,
for the demons to leave his wayward son.
The wedding went viral, and his old church
wrote him: forsake your sin or else we will...
He took "or else," and has been taking it
ever since, heeding only God, who says
always, "Trust in the Lord with all your heart
and lean not on your own understanding,"
in a voice-over like a surfer dude's.

And when those other noises, scratching hard
behind sideboards or screeching overhead,
from heaving midnight nests, bare sharp white teeth,
he thinks of his father's rat guillotine
and the sink that he proudly showed his son
to coax him into a career in medicine,
the porcelain plugged with the heads of rats.
Too grisly? Yes. Maybe. For PG-13,
he and Dickson are also daddies of kittens.

THE MUSLIM

for Zizi Azah Abdul Majid

(Ourika Café, Lower East Side, New York City, January 6, 2019)

In the soft, low hurry of her voice, I

hear why she named her daughter Zinira,

after the Roman slave so savagely

tortured for her new faith, her only God,

a scarf tightened around and in her eyes.

She was at Trader Joe's and kneeling down
for Zini's vitamins on the bottom shelf
when a Black woman cried in a loud voice,
"Why are you praying here? Stop your praying.
This is America." Once, at Columbia,
a play about the siege of Leningrad
was read in a workshop. Shocked by the news,
she asked the playwright, "Is it true, they boiled
their dead and ate the soup?" Overhearing her,
the actor, a white graduate student, smiled:
"What do you think? Those halal carts, who knows
what they put in to make the food taste good!"
The joke blindsided her. She can't forget,
standing with Zini by their car, outside
the supermarket in Connecticut,
a Jewish man wearing a Jewish hat
espying her tudung, accosted her
for her opinion on the Middle East,
the bombing of the bus in Jerusalem,
his face so close she only saw his eyes.

She took her own sweet time to go to God.
After her heart stopped in the hospital,
her grandmother woke up from her coma
a vegetative thing, dear thing, and lived
with Zizi's family for four years. Her uncle,
who went to Pearl Jam concerts with his wife
and cheered on her choice to wear the burka,
was thrown off from his motorbike and died.
She closed her show in Singapore and drove
to sit in KL with sequestered grief.
Along the drive up north and afterwards,
the question, like a supertitle, flashed—
"Why do I have to wait for someone else
to die before I take faith seriously?"

She started by praying five times a day,
pulled on long sleeves and then pulled on long pants,
smiled, frowned, smirked, narrowed her eyes at the mirror
before she ventured out, her hair well hidden.
It helped that Izmir gave her for her birthday
an Alexander McQueen headscarf, all
grinning skulls and smoky purple and brown.
She tells me this because she believes faith
is modern and because she knows I think
it's hip, a silky crown by another queen,
and will include the detail in my poem,
and so I do. She's writing a play now
about a rock band from Syria, whose faith
in music is contested by the war,
her graduate thesis on grudging theisms.

She loves New York. And Zini loves it too.
In school, she studies French and Mandarin
besides English; ethics and art as well.
She reads her storybooks when out of school,
and weaves her tapestry and plays the piano,
and when she is not doing any of these,
she writes poems. She will learn soon enough
whom she is writing for, beyond herself,
her separate and united audiences,
who grow clearer when she closes her eyes,
as her namesake praised God for blinding her
and, for returning her sight, praised Him again.

THE SAMURAI

for Zeke Allis

(Harlem Shake, New York City, February 10, 2019)

The tune found him in AP History—
the West was Wild, before the Civil War—
a cowboy tune picking its way across
a stony desert or a wary street,
hum-hammered in head until written down.
His mom and dad surmised a samurai—
too much Kurosawa—but the conceit,
the double-, no, triple-crossing crossover,
appealed to him, the "unseen prodigy"
as he described himself in middle school.
You call your teachers by Joachim or Claire
in MSC. The joke is every contest
you cannot win because nobody wins.

The Bronx High School is different. He has
more friends, more family, more enemies.
You find ways to distinguish yourself from
the pack while working your way up—a sailor
in *Anything Goes*, the Russian soloist
in *Fiddler*, kicking up a Russian storm,
and in *The Drowsy Chaperone*, finally
a principal, the groom's best man, who brings
the schoolhouse crashing down with his tap dance.
Singapore, which he visits every summer,
when the boy eats his favorite char siew noodles
and hangs out with his cousins who are bound
for medicine or engineering, Singapore
is in his childhood, also in his blood,
and makes him special to American peers
somewhat, mysterious as Doctor Who,
the show he shared with his pal Cameron,
who lives with his mom alone, as does he
in a more figurative sense, as do we.

Once he decided for the arts, his mom
decided he must make a success out of it.
She brought him the commission. He composed
from his ambiguous tune an orchestral work,
developing a part for every section,
pitching the color right for different strings,
an epic sound in the tradition of
Lord of the Rings, *Game of Thrones*, old Westerns.
He named the work *The Samurai with No Name*
after Clint Eastwood's anti-hero but
insisted at our recent interview
the work is not autobiographical.

THE ARMY REGULAR

for Thomas Nguy

(Congee Village, East Village, New York City, circa 2010)

The sons of Singapore fly from the army,
if they can, but young Thomas flew to it.
They do not want two years of hentak kaki,
marching in place, the non-action of action.
Thomas was tired of moving with his parents
from Nam to Singapore to the USA.
Reversing his atlas-spanning odyssey,
he signed up as an army regular.
At night, he heard his commanding officers
enter their men's barracks, and their men too,
their shadows flitting back and forth, like moths,
across the spotless shutters of his room.
Bastards again in the morning, they would slip
in a soft look when their recruit was looking.

THE SHIRKER

for Sandi Tan,

a montage of interview quotations

"I'm not somebody who can talk easily
to people. It's like we remembered what
it was like, to fly and now we have to walk
forever. You are back to Earth, doomed
to never speak of this because there's no
proof that it ever happened. There's no proof
you were ever special. My film *Shirkers*—
it's about me finding this lost film,
70 reels of Kodak 16mm,
in *pristine* condition. Georges had wrapped
every reel in black plastic inside their cans
and always kept them in a cool, dark place,
as if they were a gorgeous, beloved cadaver!

He was a very strange friend. He was a
great storyteller. He was very, very
talented. If he walked into the room right now,
you'd want to go off with [him]. He takes you.
No grown-up was taking me seriously.
I was the master of the stink eye. I'm
a looser tongue than most. I was the best
film critic they had back then—hah! Back then,
in the mid-to-late nineties, Singapore
had the highest rate of movie-going,
per capita, in the world—everybody
went to the movies. We, Jasmine and I,
were in a "special" high school, and it was
…basically like *X-Men Jr.* Georges
was actually a very convenient friend
for us because he was grown up, and male,
and an American. There was no way
the film equipment places were going
to give us free equipment, all this stuff.
It was because we had Georges. Georges
kept it in a room in his house, as if
it were a human. I was Laura Palmer
coming back to solve my murder all
over again. It was a huge battle.
Nobody had any faith in me, really.

I also had the paper fly me to Cannes
to watch movies and interview the Coens.
The price to pay was I also had to cover
Con Air. Moving from Singapore to the US
in my twenties, I succumbed to some shedding,
but I kept almost all of the mail I got
for *Exploding Cat*, the zine I ran when I
was sixteen—from a lonesome poet in Ohio,
an Israeli experimental musician, several
men serving life sentences in California
state prisons. Because. All these weeping kids
would come up to me after the screening.
They weren't living in cultural centers like
LA or New York, and so they were excited
to see a film that showed kids living in
the middle of nowhere and doing something
impossible. Teenagers of all ages are moved,
teenagers who are in their fifties and sixties
with unfinished projects are telling me
that now they're going to finish something.

It should be said that back in 1992,
Georges and I were obsessed with Almendros.
Inspired by him, we shot most of the original
Shirkers exteriors during magic hour,
which in equatorial Singapore lasts
only fifteen minutes. By the end of it,
it was a strange realization. I was singing
a duet with my younger self because
it's about my younger self. Learning that
I'm not fully grown up, but it's OK.
It's actually crushing to realize you've
become the grown-up that you would be
so disappointed to have grown up into.
All these weeping kids. I mean, it is *crushing*."

THE COMEDIAN

for Jocelyn Chia

(Au Bon Pain, Union Square, New York City, April 29, 2019)

He wanted her to have the world and timed

her birth in Boston, his American

beauty, three weeks before they flew back home.

Enough time, three weeks, to fly from the assault

of stodgy, singular citizenship.

In convent school, St. Nic's, the girl would crack

a classmate up until she begged for mercy.

That was so rare that she remembered it,

no, not the joking, but the laughing fit,

she tells me with the coyness of a smile.

Usually Singaporeans would um chio—
stifle a smile or smile in secret (Hokkien)—
she warns visiting comics, your A+ joke
will get a B+ laugh. Yes, yes, she grades
the laughs she gets, how loud, how hard, how long,
how much the bodies spasm, how much crying.
Best joke in Singapore? She posts next gig,
American friends write: *you go, girl.*
Singapore friends: *can get free tickets har?*

Best joke anywhere? First time she made out

with an American dude, the boy whooped,

who's your daddy? who's your daddy? and

thinking he needed an internship, answered,

Antony Chia. She has since honed the joke

on her to a sharp point. The punchline lands,

six years later, *you're my father, you're my father.*

And now she thinks she has a killer add.

Do you think, she asks me, Singaporeans

will bawl over this new turn of the screw,

if I say, quitting my lawyering job

for comedy was like going to war,

do you think they will get PTSD?

THE ART DIRECTOR

for Mark Yeo

(Madam Zhu's Kitchen, West Village, New York City, October 24, 2019)

Not knowing the West Village was Manhattan,
for months the naif longed to see Manhattan.
The fucking bimbo! If Abby threw him out,
his plan was to bus tables and live in the Bronx
under the railway tracks. Always exploring
he was, meeting the crazies and the druggies
in Williamsburg, running home from the bus,
terrified of being mugged or worse. Ten dollars
his daily budget—thank you, Chinese takeouts—
and once he busted it on *Mission Impossible.*

But he knew, *knew*, he was in the right place.
The parties, for one, where his habiliment,
once a headgear topped by a cymbal-clapping
windup monkey for a Moroccan party,
never let down his hosts, attracting chatter,
shutters, and eyelash flutters. For another,
after ten letters a day and cold-calling,
the job offers came in with a green card.
(They loved his light box of a portfolio.)
For yet another, the boy would have died
in Singapore, according to the doctors
who blamed the weather for mystery sicknesses,
and there were signs, so many fucking signs,
not in the stars but in *Star Wars*, big things
awaiting the foolhardy, the resistance,
who scored As in all subjects but F9
in Engrish; who were the last families
to leave their old kampong in Yio Chu Kang,
hating the Death Star of a HDB block,
and, sure enough, the mutt Ah Fat next day
died of heartbreak; who were protected by
a gui ren, the Jedi of a dead grandfather,
until they learned to stand up for themselves

and say, I speak slowly only for your sake.
If you don't understand my accent, ah,
I feel sorry for you, but I wun change.
According to my family, it's our fate
to be together in this life and place,
so live the max and make the best of it
for once. For we will never meet again.

THE PHILOSOPHER

for Cheng-Wei Chin

(Magnolia Bakery, Upper West Side, New York City, March 18, 2019)

Capitalism will wither away,

my friend assures me, as technology

reduces the cost of making anything

to nothing, and we will work as we please.

After quitting Wall Street a year ago,

he had time to think. The universal,

what is true at all times and in all places,

occupies him. And capitalism

has a beginning and, no doubt, an end,

unlike the desire for equality.

He looks at me with meaning, and I am

once more the LGBT activist.

I almost ask about the struggle for status,

is that not universal too. I don't.

Here is someone I knew in my lost youth,

in long-ago Officer Cadet School

and luckily recovered in New York.

How is the laughing boy soldier related

to this, the sober philosopher? He looks the same,

hair black, the narrow face, big eyes,

still handles himself with robotic grace.

As if he read my thoughts, my friend goes on,

he does not think we have a self, if by

a self we mean a thing that stays the same.

Our cells, beliefs, our memories, they change

throughout our lives and arbitrarily,

and what we call our self is what remains

when death discontinues the changing change.

We talk about several other things,

but these things stay with me after we say

goodbye outside Magnolia Bakery.

In the spring air, a chill not there before

marches me smartly to my uptown train.

THE ARCHITECT

for Christopher Chew

(Rasa Malaysian Restaurant, West Village, New York City, September 4, 2019)

The funeral bells, the roadside operas—
Sago Lane was too noisy for his studies
and so his parents shipped him to a flat
in the East Coast, bought with the steaming blood
of slaughtered chickens squawking in big barrels.
Business dropped after they were relocated
from street to basement of Smith Street Complex,
as part of the cleanup of Chinatown,
and the construction of the train station began.
He did his A-levels in KFC,
it could be said, he did it in air-con,
and chose his field for the six years it gave
to decide what to do. Or not to do.

He was quite lost and over-overworked
till Tan Hock Beng took him under his wing
and taught the kid, for the first time, to think.
The World of Architecture at Beijing,
a communist showcase, single-handedly
he edited into a monograph.
Back in NUS, his final-year project,
a movie theater, with an outré poster,
was graded F by the local examiner,
and by the Brit and Yankee, a high A.
The way was clear: go where they understand.
He was not the only one to get such grades
and choose to go abroad, but he went alone
not to the Strand but to Sesame Street,
where Big Bird made Columbia feel like home,
and where he read the original writings
of Frank Lloyd Wright and of Le Corbusier.
"If it's not in English," said the eight-foot-tall
canary, "find a way to learn the language."

And so he did, with all his indigenous
understandings and misunderstandings,
studied, worked, and built in America
its retail stores and private residences,
its home, head, haute, and start-up offices,
until he had to cancel his annual visit
to Singapore because of a bully boss,
found himself again over-overworked.
Time, he thought, to take a sabbatical.
He quit his job and made his quiet way
through Kenneth Frampton's bibliography, big
as it was, searching out the inclinations,
priorities, and changes in the thinking
of this woke expat historian from Woking.
How far could "critical regionalism" go,
this idea of synthesizing two forces,
modernity—science, tech, democracy—
and nervous, fervid, louche vernaculars,
the universals and pre-universals?
Skyscrapers say nothing about a people,
but there's no return to Tudor cottages,
Chris clarified, impaling the steamed chicken
before dipping it in the chili sauce.
I had another bowl of rice. He did not.

The danger is nostalgia and not just
the warp-speed development of Singapore.
Petitions to keep up People's Park Complex,
William Lim's interpretation of Unité,
were mounted, but how many petitioners
would live there? Not the parents of his friend
who suffer lift breakdowns and fire hazards.
Neither a sculpture nor a dinosaur,
for the art market or the history museum,
a building should respond to human needs,
or else it is another worthless Vessel,
and as the architect in Chris continued
way past the friend's typical reticence,
a twist on an old poem turned my mind,
a poem itself a twist on an old idiom—
a building should be renovated like
a nest, for chickens to come home to roost.

THE CHEF

for Richard Chan

(Yummy Tummy, Flushing, New York City, March 24, 2019)

Unctuously fried oyster omelet.

Hainanese chicken rice. Sambal fish balls

pierced on a stick, as in the old night markets,

airborne kerosene lamps lisping with a flair.

Mee goreng with sliced fish cake, Chinese sausage

and egg. Bak kut teh spelled the correct way,

the way of memory, for bone meat tea.

And finally, the chef's very own favorite,

the pièce de résistance, on which he lavished

a fiery, slurry, egg tomato sauce,

the chilli crab, made from Dungeness crabs,

in which we dig with fingers for sweet flesh.

The critics got him wrong. He has not changed

profession. He is still a travel agent.

THE SPECULATIVE FICTION WRITER

for Manish Melwani

(Rasa Malaysian Restaurant, West Village, New York City, March 25, 2019)

Would Partition had not birthed two babies,
one named what was, the other what could be,
because the family then found itself
torn in two, between staying and going,
and followed finally the Sindhi way,
teleporting all to Morocco, Burma,
and, in his dada's case, to Singapore.

Would he, Manish Melwani, at his maths
had scored and had not been turfed (luckily!)
from Anglo-Chinese to American,
where Mr. Silverman showed him the art
of penning science fiction, of building worlds,
man-eating flowers, fantastic egg-shaped mounds,
nor taken on the rap of gangsta chic,
under the influence of Wu-Tang Clan,
and drunk on weekends with the sonabitches
who never gave him time of day but now
hung out with him, guardian of the gateway
to girls, the jagar of their Shangri-La,
because out of despair's hairy armpit
he rode the winged creature, confidence,
to summer school at the Jack Kerouac
and worked with Chip, who tore apart his novel
but recommended him to Clarion.
There, the unreal encounter with real friends
and the embodiment of love. The call,

there, to drop advertising for authorship,
copywriting for writing. There. Would Wells,
Clarke, Asimov, and the other grandmasters
had breathed diversity into their aliens,
would Herbert had not modeled Arrakis
on Iraq, because the alien trope exerted
a stranglehold on our imagination.
Speculations flower from the soil of facts.
They become facts. Back home in Singapore,
the Aljunieds, the great trading Yemenis,
who lived in Malaya even before Raffles,
are quizzed about where they come from, as if
only the Chinese are Singaporeans.
Tharman, the best person to lead the country,
is declared unelectable because
Singapore is not ready for an Indian
prime minister, for such an oxymoron.
It is enough to turn anyone's head
egg-white with grief or to a raging pyre.
The casual slurs—man, can't you take a joke—
downed at house parties with a whiskey neat,
the house plants baring their titanium teeth.

Entering NS with the Poly batch,
he left the champagne bubble when he met
Punjabi boys whose fathers drove the taxis
he liked to imagine as time machines,
whose mothers cleaned the hospitals, the boys
already men in trials of wit and strength.
His gray enciks, who happened to be Sikhs,
warned him against joining the army—he
would hentak kaki as a captain forever
while junior officers, some whom he trained,
who happened to be Chinese, got promoted.
Two worlds. Three. Four. He was in Singapore

when Sakthivel Kumaravelu died

under the wheels of a bus on Race Course Road,

and fellow workers, most from Tamil Nadu,

smashed the offensive vehicle that whisked

them out of sight to tight and spartan dorms,

overturned police cars, set them on fire,

threw bottles, rocks, eggplants at Special Ops.

He was the men who struck the ambulance

and also was the men in yellow vests

who stumbled out of it, hands shielding heads,

making a desperate run for safety. Would

Sinnathamby Rajaratnam, sometimes
he had thought while composing in New York
his paper on the Third World for the panel
at the third SLF, would the deputy
prime minister had stayed a fiction writer
in London, a writer noticed by George Orwell,
a writer with a deep love for the poor,
a writer who would have imagined him,
instead of turning his pen hand to power,
bringing a nation, not a novel, to
Being. Reality. Would he. Would he.

THE EDITOR

for Kimberley Lim,

engaged to Joel Pitra on August 25, 2019, four years to the day when they first met

She did not want to date white guys. She did
not want to date at all, loving the icy flavor
of keeping to herself the soul's good news.
An editing job led her to New York
and into Pret a Manger where a voice
hailed her, "You're Singaporean, let's be friends,
I can tell from your accent." It was Chun.
Invited to a movie in Central Park,
she met Chun's latest friend, a guy called Joel.

He was not Singaporean, and she
turned up her nose at the news: vegetarian.
Strikingly tall, and white, he played paintball
and every weekend trained in jiu-jitsu.
Watching the movie *Fame*, which overcame
her strong distaste for all things popular—
the young filling the pages of their lives
with such a sweet, naive, and awkward beauty
she wanted to take a red pen to it—
she, unlike Chun, did not speak much to Joel,
and so the next-day text *I'd like to get
to know you better* raised a red flag.
She sent a snarky reply back, and he
wrote again, and she put him off again.
A week of intermittent messages
before agreeing to attend with him
Chun's dance concert, gelato earlier.
When she insisted on paying for both
Italian treats, adding for his pride's sake,
"since she was late," freely he let her pay,
and a chill stole into her, silly thought,
her dad would never have let her mom pay.

First night at Joel's place, in Ridgewood,
they slept, both fully clothed, in the same bed,
to beat the chill, she added in her comments
on a first draft of this poem, mine and hers.
The night became a test, for many nights,
to pass by failing or to fail by passing.
Yet "test" sounds "too hard" (in my self-edit),
it sounds "just wrong" (in hers). This was a sense
more sensitive and more mysterious,
as if between the sheets, a common womb,
something was growing, lungs first, and then heart,
a face, a brain, as if between the lines,
a meaning would finally be discerned.

And what the meaning means, no one can see,

but every time I see them walking off,

Joel so tall and Kimberley so short,

I bless what they have made of inequality.

THE PRODIGAL

for Justin Chin (1969–2015)

He took his fortune on the road—a toke
of toxic stories, like the moths in May
so easily swatted into pure asbestos.
Hawaii was the first stop, but SF
beckoned with its buff fags and druggy poets,
Tom Sellecks into golden showers while
reciting Les Fleurs du fucking mal.
To use the body up, disintegrate
into the yellow shards of the forsythia,
to savor the next day the rally, slow
and painstaking, of muscle, bone, and blood
in morning muck and in the sty of style
was well worth living for, dying for, even.

How proud he was, the prodigal, when he
hit upon making the mom watch her son,
she hazy with Alzheimer's, he with coke,
receive the shit unreeling from his trick
into his mouth, like a communion wafer,
while she disposes, satchel after satchel,
sugar into hers, scattering stray crystals
onto her front, transforming her housedress
into the sequined gown of a drag queen.
There is no turning point in Justin's story,
no moment when the son came to his senses
(he was already living through his senses),
not even when he got his diagnosis.

Just this: you're watching TV with your dad,

about the water parks in the Middle East,

and the man makes a mess due to his meds.

When he gets up quietly, without a word,

to change his clothes and find the air freshener,

you look ahead, you do not turn your head,

at the fun waterslide, long as a mile,

with jets so powerful they can propel

a half-pint up and back from where he came.

THE PORN STAR

for Annabel Chong (fl. 1994–2003)

Who killed Annabel Chong, I hear you ask.
Her mother, when she tied the babysitter,
a handkerchief, to the kindergartner's front
to swipe away her where-is-mummy tears.
The trauma, opined the female critic, emptied
Annabel for all the dicks in her porn career.
That's why the porn star wished in self-delusion
to make her parents proud, as mum was proud
her daughter rubbed the faces of her friends,
crying their hearts out, with the stitch of fabric.

She was an overachiever, a gifted kid,
and like so many of her eighties cohort
killed off her inhibitions once abroad.
Half drunk, one night, alone, in London town,
she followed off the train a smiling man.
(Me too, late in the naughts, right off the PATH
into a cozy home in Hoboken.
He came, I had not, but was ushered out
into the empty city. To this day,
I still remember the Munch reproductions.)
The Brit raped her, and in the unlit alley
appeared his lads, from god knows where, and had
their turn, orderly as at a lunch counter.

Did she die then? Was it a ghost of vengeance

who flew to LA and filmed with football jocks

"I Can't Believe I Did the Whole Team,"

flanked by the furies of two Asian sisters?

LA, Hugh Hefner's playground and capital.

If Armageddon hit the world, she thought

in movie terms, it would begin in LA.

Cupped in the hills above Hollywood,

the sets of an engorged porn industry,

the disused warehouses and private homes

through which the touted milk of human kindness—

directors, actors, and crew members—spurted.

Here Annabel met John T. Bone and made
her mark, bossed by the man from Manchester.
"The World's Biggest Gang Bang" shot her to fame.
A porno arms race, post–Cold War, took off—
who could shoot more, buy more, sell more, take more.
Billed as 300 men, really 70,
all shapes and sizes, colors, looks, and ages,
committed 251
sex acts with the porn star Annabel Chong.
Unknown to her, not all of them were tested
for HIV, not all attested clean.
Between a colonnade of phalluses,
fake Doric columns, plaster Venuses
in various states of undress interspersed,
a garden worthy of a Messalina
in Hollywood, the would-be lovers snaked
and, five at a time, mounted the platform,
blue with a polyester tarp, and tupped
the self-identifying "female stud."

Mr. T. Bone, at a water break, asked her,

"Annabel, what makes you such a sexual monster?"

He never paid her, although he made a killing.

He did not kill her. She tested negative,

and after acting and directing some,

including the gangbang film *Pornomancer*,

her take on William Gibson's novel, she

got fucking bored of fucking with Annabel.

She took a job in IT, announced it

the vile work of the Evil Doppelgänger.

Uncannily, refusing to be canned,

Annabel Chong was primed for resurrection

by heroin addict and mommy's boy

Gough Lewis, whose doco on Annabel

provided some material for this poem.

He never got "The World's" a parody,

a para-ode, beside the fucking point.

I quote from a late interview she gave:

"Sometimes I'd be talking about sex,"

Annabel said, "in a more philosophical

way, and he wouldn't really understand."

How then could such a man edit her ideas

when she had always done the cutting herself?

One of the film producers Suzanne Whitten

renamed the film "Sex: the Gough Lewis Story

told by Gough Lewis through Annabel Chong."

The gaffe by Gough. You see the irony?

The subject turns out to be the subject,

even from the beginning of the world,

the Word with God, was God, and all that jizz.

One man at the big bang was trying to get
into the business. Another, from New York,
was there for the adventure. The third wanted
to be a part of history. Middle-aged
and balding, the fourth man on camera
was holding a red rose in a plastic sheath.
All left me just looking. A ragged bloom
I raised, unbidden, when a cute young blond
kneeled down to eat her cunt as the Empress,
deathless as digital storage, one and zero,
clumsily removed her gold lamé dress.

THE DYING NURSE

1. Pera Mediterranean Brasserie, Midtown,

New York City, June 27, 2018

I did not wish to write this book, no, ma'am,

having no genius for composing right

a narrative, even with incidents

and characters provided by your life.

I had no interest in the lives of others,

not really, but in their effect on me,

the sun striking the sea in distant diamonds,

and so I recommended another pen,

Singaporean too, Amanda Lee Koe,

who composed *Ministry of Moral Panic.*

Good title, right? Compare with *Steep Tea.*

One story, in particular, about

an older woman befriending a schoolgirl,

presenting her the world, á la Aladdin,

before the girl found out her friend was married

and dying soon, would speak to you. It did,

but you insisted on speaking to me,

whom you would later introduce to friends

as your boy toy or therapist or else

your mother's bastard son, newly found out.

I'll call you Linda P. You were a nurse,

and you are dying for sure of breast cancer,

and so I left behind the sparkly sea

and climbed uphill into another country.

There are as many ways, said Linda P,

of handling death as there are people dying.

She ate another spoon of her steel-cut

oatmeal while my glass emptied its corkscrew

for a third Bellini. It was early still.

The restaurant held us only, as if all

the saints had left the earth for saintly bliss.

Lucky for us, the waiter stayed as well

and brought my drink, Linda continuing

by a diversion. Her boss, a Russian Jew,

married a Brooklyn Methodist, but for

practical purposes at Sloan Kettering

was married to his head nurse, Linda P.

Not seeing he was having a hard day,

his handsome face tighter than a knot,

she practiced on the brain surgeon a joke

culled from a patient's call: What's the difference
between a New York and a Florida Jew?
He snapped, this gentle, patient man and friend.
It goes to show you never know a man,
or woman, how they would react to death
even after a great deal of great dealings.
Twenty years of working for Felix G.
Some marriages don't last so long. Before
her mother hooked her father, she had another
husband, the son of a Thai prince, some said.
The princeling drank and, worse, gambled away
whole buildings. Then he died mysteriously.
Some said, the family had it in for him.
Her second husband died when Linda was two,
survived a war but not a heart attack.
Her mother buried him in the cemetery
and her cash closer, down in the back garden,
freshly turned soil the only sign of mania.
Linda inherited his asthma. The war
against her dad inside of her was fought
by the wrong method, daily adrenalin shots,
no physical activity, they said.
We know better now—we should walk and play.
Back in those days, the restless fifties, sixties,
there were prescriptions for all kinds of things
if you belonged to a particular class.

The country clamored for Merdeka—Freedom!—
at rallies, sit-ins, work stoppages, strikes,
but her feet were not allowed to touch the floor
till she turned three, in the big house at Katong,
and she was chauffeured everywhere she went,
one reason, perhaps, why she walked away
from her first husband, born with a silver spoon,
like her. And you threw it away, her mother railed.
His name was David T, the sweetest man.
They met at a friend's eighteenth birthday party,
a diamonded affair on Broadrick Road,
and, in true fairy-tale style, he fell for her,
told his parents to cancel, like a check,
the next day's meeting with the matchmaker,
for which Linda's in-laws would not forgive her.
When David's mom consulted the oracle
about her daughter's marriage, the fat crone,
a fortune-teller famous in the country,
turned to Linda instead and, staring hard,
foretold in Mandarin the end of her marriage.
David's mom translated it with a face
that was far harder to read than the future.
What climbed into my mind (ours?) but unspoken
in Davio's was the wild and sneaky thought
that fate was pre-arranged by mommy dearest.
(Here Linda remembered another crone,

earlier, but no place came back to mind,
who warned that she would lose a darling child
if she walked out of an arranged marriage.)
For sure Linda fulfilled the prophecy:
before a year was up, she left for London,
for further studies, David let it be known.
She could not live without the luxuries
of Singapore, he thought. More girl than woman,
she would return to the comfort of love,
the family duty, and the wedding vow.
She proved him wrong by moving to New York,
but for years, he sent money and visited
her mom weekly and gave her money too.
She took the cash and hid it in the garden
where the Japs couldn't find the strongboxes,
but she never forgave David for signing
the papers that gave his wife, not twenty-one,
a husband's legal consent to leave home.
When the cancer came home and from the dugs
migrated to other parts, Linda chose
not chemo but hormonal therapy.
She wished to live out her remaining years
in relative comfort and ease of movement.
Chemo would crush not only her but John,
and she couldn't bear to live with someone
who was in so much pain. She would have left

her second husband. Her proxy who
refused to pull the plug when it was time.
His job was to help people to breathe and not
to take away the breath of life, he argued.
To which Linda P cried in frustration,
why do you want to be my proxy, John,
when you can't do what I want? No reply.
Her fellow nurses said, we will do it
when he is not looking. Linda said this
with a sense of humor and a touch of pride.
You can see humor in everything.
She counseled once a grief-stricken man
whose wife was dying in her ward, and he
begged to have sex with Nurse—he was
so horny. Of course, she turned down his offer.
The husband next: can you come to the wake?
Her colleagues joked that Linda slept with all
the right people, so well she got along
with patients, doctors, and administrators.
True, once a handsome doctor hit on her.
Stanley, aren't you married? she said. He said,
my wife is married, but I am not.
She laughed. She had used the line herself
but only in flirtation, never for real,
until she met Brian O. Afterwards,
for years, he sent postcards of all his travels,

every sight expressing the wish to see her,

top of the Eiffel or down the Colosseum,

postcards sent through the care of the hospital,

postcards she read but never did reply.

One card wended its fateful way to John,

who worked in Respiratory, and he

gave Brian her email. Linda never asked

what John thought he was doing, not ever.

Some things are better accepted as gifts.

To put Brian off, she wrote he could see her

when she retired, and so when she retired,

from County Cork the knight came to New York.

By this time, we were walking to the trains,

and every body and soul, back from heaven,

weaving the discarded rope of life again,

bore not a mark of bliss but an intent

to go about the day's appointed business.

3. Linda P's house, Croton-on-Hudson,

New York, January 3, 2019

Come for lunch, Linda P invited me,

and see my favorite haunt, the Croton Dam.

At the green foot, a park, the masonry rose

majestically like a castle wall,

the tallest dam at the time when it was built,

while next to it, through a hidden spillway,

a licensed breach, the Croton River stormed

down flinty rocks and boulders scattered here

and there to make of the tall waterfall

a replica of ruin's wasteful entrance.

The picture changes, Linda P observed,

according to the seasons. Now it's full

of swagger, then it suffers like a cat,

some days it is the calmest thing I know.

Back in her car, she spoke about her luck.

She had knocked down all four poles at the test,

and yet the tester passed her. Singapore

just had to meet its quotas, she had thought.

At Rego Park, the cop who stopped her car

was baffled by her foreign license. Quickly,

she told him she was leaving the USA

the next day, and he let her go, relieved.

She had lived all over New York, Forest Hills,

St. Mark's Place, East 5th Street, East 71st,

and moved, with John, to Croton in '87.

The house, last of a townhouse apartment block,

looked more modest than I had imagined,

the inside tidy and clean, a nurse's home.

Lunch is almost ready, Linda P said,

we're having siew mai and popiah. Look around.

The cats that greeted us had disappeared,

leaving behind photos and pencil drawings
of a handsome predecessor on the walls.
Linda married John with her hair down,
a wedding photo showed, looking much younger
than when she wedded David and his diamonds.
A snapshot of an adolescent boy
in high-school sweats and jeans, a handsome kid.
My son, Tatum, Linda said. Lunch is ready.
She made the sambal belacan from scratch,
pounding shrimp paste and red chilies by hand
while watching TV. No calamansi lime,
that hybrid of kumquat and mandarin,
so lemon had to do, a substitute
sufficiently good to quell the spiciness.
Before I moved away, Linda P said,
I didn't know houses didn't come with servants.
My image of my mom was seeing her
reading English romance novels all day
while rocking slowly in her rocking chair.
When she stayed with me, she was so shocked
to see me busy in the kitchen. Once,
she lost a ring and blamed the cleaning lady,
a Black grandma from Brooklyn, made a fuss,
before finding the diamond in the fridge,
where dear mama had hidden it from the help.
A governess brought up her three daughters;

she had a son, but no one knew his fate.
The boy was born the day the father died,
very bad luck. A servant took him, some said,
out of the house and never came back.
Some said, mom gave the baby to the servant.
In any case, mother died with her secrets,
and now I am free to dig all around.
Clear through the kitchen window, uncleared woods
where a wild deer, or two, would appear,
even approach the house, with its slim face.
Brian came to Croton that year; it was April,
the year of her retirement from work.
He was four years younger than Linda P
but had the looks of someone ten years younger.
He hit it off with John. Both of them loved
a garden, a patch claimed from wilderness,
and built together that long wooden block
to stop the rain from washing the soil away,
a kind of dam, you might say, but for land.
The hydrangeas are thriving. In the spring,
you can see, Linda P said, they will sport
two kinds of flowers, mopheads and lacecaps,
a sea of pink and blue and lavender.
Since then, she had seen Brian every year,
Ireland in '17, Valencia
last year, and Paris with Brian's daughter too.

She loved to travel, and it was a thrill
to be another man's girlfriend again,
or, more accurately, her own once more.
After having foie gras, Linda P that night
woke up with a sharp pain in her chest.
Stupidly she had forgotten to bring her meds,
and Paris at night did not sell aspirin,
as Brian found out, dashing from store to store.
The chest pain ebbed away but not the fright
for him. If something were to happen to you,
what am I supposed to say to your husband?
She said, I had a lot of time to think,
and I've concluded that it's not my problem.
She laughed at the memory of saying such
a thing and helped me to the last siew mai.
Paris is not such a bad way to go.
She often wondered what John made of her
seeing her platonic lover once a year;
she did not think that she would stand for it
if John were seeing an ex regularly.
It is unfair, she readily admitted,
but it is an unfairness of long standing,
holding up the waters that feed a city,
on the west side a park for families,
submerged hillsides and tillage on the east.
In their life together, John does the right thing,

and she does the thing that is right for her,
but matters are not so easily sorted
when the right thing is the thing right for you
and the thing right for you is the right thing.
After the visit to Ireland, she knew
she would not leave her New York life for Brian.
She had a wonderful time, and Brian's daughters
were very kind, one telling her the password
to his iPad was "I love Linda," but
three weeks in Limerick convinced her
that she had not lost anything. And yet,
after the visit to Ireland, she told John,
I want to keep seeing Europe with Brian.
If you're not happy, you can walk away.
He was so shocked that he did walk away,
but only to the kitchen and from the fridge
opened the bottle tops she couldn't open,
of sambal, sesame oil, sweet soy sauce,
because of spinal stenosis, the nerve
pinched by the narrowing of the canal.
John runs marathons—the last at Death Valley—
and has the marathoner's grace of pacing
and outpacing other runners in the race,
or so I thought about why he had stayed.
You must meet him, Linda said, and my friends,
but you mustn't say you're writing about me

because I want them to be natural,

to speak openly. No real names to be used.

And you will split the profit of the book,

fifty for you to enjoy and have fun,

fifty for the foundation for my son.

From the window ledge the maneki-neko

beckoned and beckoned with its swinging paw.

There's not much money in poetry, I said.

She said, whatever you can get for the story.

On Tatum's twelfth birthday, Linda took him

to a fancy restaurant where the boy proceeded

to order the most expensive steak.

When you're invited somewhere, choose what you like,

Linda advised her son, but you don't have

to choose the cheapest or the most expensive

if you want to be invited again. But, Mom,

he said, I have inherited your taste.

He was good at spending his parents' money,

and they let him, so charmed they were by their son.

But he did not spend it all on himself.

When on a short visit, an aunt lavished a gift,

he took his pal to Amsterdam. Generous

he was to a fault with his many girlfriends,

who still kept in touch with Linda and John

after his death. Tatum was living in Queens,

while studying law at St. John's in Hillcrest,

when they did not hear from him for a week.
John went to his studio in Jackson Heights
and found the bathroom sealed with plastic sheets
and duct tape neatly, without a breach,
a warning sign put up for first responders.
The fumes were made from household chemicals,
I later learned. In the first half of 2008,
five hundred Japanese men, women, and children
followed an online recipe to mix
bath sulfur with a toilet bowl cleaner
and slipped away into the breach at home.
How did John find his son, dressed or undressed,
I wished to ask, thinking of Tatum's sweats
and our self-presentation at the last,
but I knew not to pry but to wait for more.
The Japanese cat waved. Linda P said,
He never had a summer job, no need,
but was a great worker once he was in.
The summer before college, I got him
a job working in the local hardware store.
The boss was full of praise, his thoughtfulness,
his quick initiative, the discipline
from hours of training on the tennis court.
Running late one day, Tatum took a cab,
but not to work; he passed the store, went north

along the Hudson to god knows where.
I found out from the bill how much he spent
but never where he went. Put down the plates,
I will clear them, but you must catch your train.
It takes ten minutes to drive to the station.
With luck, you'll make it. In the waiting room,
Linda continued in the car, the women
waiting for their hormonal therapy
all want to talk, but I don't want to talk
about treatments and curious lumps and doctors.
There was this woman looking stricken, once,
and so I engaged her, and it turned out
that she did not know how to tell her son
who was getting married to his college sweetheart.
The world is divided into two types of people,
Linda P said, entering the parking lot,
those who give a shit and those who don't.
Why give a shit for those who don't? Cancer
will tell you who's who, that's its saving grace.
My train back to Manhattan was pulling in,
and, with a quick peck on her cheek, I flew.
Is this it? A son's suicide? The house key?

Sitting across from Linda P, I thought,
when should I bring up Tatum, but instead
was treated to a lengthy disquisition
on the art of organizing a tag sale.
The ladies of Asbury United Methodist,
under the leadership of Linda P,
would raise eight thousand dollars annually
from selling toys, electronics, and stuff
someone discarded and someone regarded
a bargain. The sale involved a lot of work,
from sorting and throwing out the worthless things
(but not in front of the donors) to washing
in warm soapy water the fine glassware,
and Linda P was ready to hand it over
to a successor capable of success.
She could not stand the insecurity
of leaders who, once gone, must still be mourned.
She had replaced others, and, in due course,
at the right time, she too would be replaced.
The idea, if that indeed was what it was,
was bred into her very genes, her father
usurping the tall place of the Thai princeling.
When she took her nursing exam in Singapore,

she wasn't a good student, so her mother
went to see a bomoh, a witch doctor,
and said to Linda when she came home, smiling,
don't worry, everything's been taken care of.
The results came out. Linda passed, but a girl
whom everyone expected to pass failed.
I took her place, and that was why I passed.
Each time John hears the story, he asks tartly,
how much money did your mother give
to the examiners, and I would not,
could not, reply. I don't understand it,
so how could I explain it to a white guy?
Passing the driving test was such a fix,
I found out later, but not this exam.
There was no quota to meet, so there was
no reason not to pass the two of us.
Another thing. When my mother was young,
she had wanted to be a nurse, and when
she didn't, she wanted it for me instead.
I took her place too, and now I am,
in some way, living out her fantasy.
I joined Sloan Kettering in the same year
as Diamond and Alyssa, all of us
starting with the night shift, but my boss liked me,
and so I got the day shift faster.
It doesn't matter, my friends said, my friends

of thirty years, you don't obey the rules.
You must meet them, and they will tell you
every terrible thing I've done and said.
When I was floating, easier than team nursing,
Diamond's patient gave me an expensive gift—
a pair of pearl earrings—although the patient
had been with Diamond for a while. She complained.
I said to her, well, did you sleep with him?
She did not like the joke. She and Alyssa
had placed me in a group I did not think
I was in. When Alyssa went with me
to Singapore, my New York friends asked me
how she was treated over there, and I
was taken aback. I had never thought of her
as Black. Was I naive, willful, or what?
Tatum always said—here I leaned forward—
that he inherited all my bad points
and all his dad's good points. He was always
getting into trouble and out of it.
After he died, when? February 10, 2010,
I attended several support groups,
each one depressingly the same as the last.
The other kids who died were doing drugs,
heroin, cocaine, and crystal meth.
They all had sad but believable stories,
but not Tatum. He was bullshitting the group

as he did when alive, so charmingly.
He loved so easily, and he was loved
for the ease all his friends found with themselves
when with him. He had the gift for living.
When he killed himself, he was dating Grace
from law school and was found holding her
photograph in his hand. There was no note.
Have I told you that Tatum wrote poems?
He wrote poems, but he did not leave a note,
as if he had run out of words at last.
My son out of words. Unbelievable.
After saying goodbye at Grand Central,
her elegant black figure, vividly scarfed
at the throat, vanishing into the crowd,
I thought I should have asked to see his poems,
but what could they be but sentimental scribblings
just to purchase the hearts of a sweetheart
and of a doting mother. I turned down
42nd and walked toward Times Square.
Good for a tag sale but not for Broadway.

5. Lexington Brass, Midtown East,
New York City, May 19, 2019

There are three turning points in my charmed life,
said Linda P helpfully, three big ones.

The first was when I walked out on David T
and ran away from Singapore, the cage,
the gilded cage for women of a class.
It was the biggest decision of my life.
It seemed so then, and so it seems right now.
The second turn happened when Tatum died,
and everything was subject to questioning.
The third was Brian O's return to me.
Just here, our server came back and ushered us
from the jam-packed bar to an empty table
before Linda continued. The cancer, both
the first time and the second, was a shock,
but it did not change a thing deep inside.
It only intensified what was already there.
But Brian…after forty-two years of working,
of serving others, I had just retired
without making any plans for retirement,
and here arrived an unexpected change
of scenery. In Charleville, in Cork,
a town so small it has only one main street,
Brian's family owns the hardware shop,
a bar called O, and the funeral parlor.
I have told you how warm and welcoming
his daughters were on my first visit.
His younger brother was the same, whisking me

out for big dinners every other night.
They have become a real family to me.
I am alone in New York, besides John.
One sister lives in Australia, the other
in Toronto before she died of breast cancer.
Yes, it runs in the family. My niece,
who has nine kids in Toronto, has it too.
So, to be welcomed into a family
is a real blessing, a family who knows
how to work hard and play even harder
and how to die for the old family business.
I love visiting them, but I can't live there.
You can lie to anyone because it does not
really matter, but you can't lie to yourself.
So the turning point was this: I asked myself
when I was flying back, could I live there?
Hell, no! Now I know where my place is.
I can see myself leaving my husband more
than I can see myself leaving New York,
where you can always find a jam-packed bar
and an empty table.

6. Text Message,

May 20, 2019

I want you

to meet my fake daughter and my fake son.

7. Wagamama, Midtown,

New York City, July 29, 2019

I had just returned from Singapore,

having seen that my mom was doing fine,

piecing her life back after my dad's death,

when Linda asked to meet. Short but erect,

she wore her chiffon dress like a second skin,

moss green, the lines torqued by a bias cut.

I paid her style a compliment. She flushed.

Have you seen the movie *The Farewell*,

Linda P asked, after ordering our lunch;

I can't get the opening line out of my mind.

It's all based on a lie sums up my life.

The character played by Awkwafina—you

know she's from Queens—goes back to China

for a fake wedding but really to say goodbye

to her grandma who doesn't know she's dying.

The movie made me so homesick right there

in the posh theater built in Pleasantville

from a donation by a millionaire.
It's all based on a lie, and that's my life.
I'm not supposed to run so far away
from Singapore, I'm not supposed to lose
a son, I'm not supposed to love again,
but here I am, living a lying truth.
I haven't told you about Disney World.
Do you know Naomi H? No? The author
of many books about the low-carb diet.
A young doctor was trying to discharge her,
but they couldn't agree on the discharge plan.
When you're on steroids, you need to taper down
the dose, but she wouldn't have the tapering.
I was called in, and I rewrote a little
the taper in the way she wanted it,
and she was happy. Not the resident.
He asked, who are you? and I said, take it
or leave it, it's your choice. All my friends say,
you know how to say fuck off so politely.
The doctor's tone irked me, the clear contempt,
so dismissive, of young doctors for nurses.
In their orientation program, they would
be told, if you have any problems, go
to Linda P and don't you question her.
I'm known around the hospital as God.
After Naomi was discharged, she kept up

with me and invited Alyssa and me
to Disney World, Orlando. We flew there
and had a marvelous time. All the rides,
no lines. Naomi just waved her VIP.
Space Mountain, Under the Sea, Magic Carpets.
Naomi said, you don't have to stand in line
for, guess what, It's a Small World after all.

8. *The Mermaid Inn, East Village,*
New York City, August 20, 2019

I don't go by the prices, Linda said,
reading the long menu. If it's expensive,
it does not mean it's good. Instead, I like
to go by whether I like it or not.
John's parents used to give me bottles of wines,
good ones, and now I can't settle for worse.
I used to pop over to my next-door neighbor
for a five-minute visit and a nip,
and I would tell John, keep on texting me
if your wife doesn't return in half an hour.
Every year, we spend a week in Maine,
with John's sister-in-law who has remarried,
big parties, dinners and drinks, on Deer Isle.
She works as a life coach for Hollywood actors
and turned Justin T around from his slump.

To all her billionaire clients who crave fame,
she asks the same thing, you need to tell me
what makes you get up in the morning. What
surprisingly varied, and buried, the answers.
On the last visit, and all visits could be last,
it was low tide, and from the house, the stretch
of beach uncovered by the sea's retreat
beckoned. She asked her son, thirteen years old,
to walk with me out to the setting sun.
The young man chivalrously took my hand,
and we walked noiselessly on the wet sand,
the distant diamonds tinkling in my ear,
until he put a question to me, why,
if you can say, did you leave Singapore?
I said, to understand, you need to be
twice your age, then I will come back to you.
I was so flattered he was interested.
Then he said, I can't figure out your accent,
this boy, who lives in cities by the sea,
with a white mother and a Black father,
who learned of Mexico from his babysitter,
now wishing, with his wits, to pin me down,
as If the world needs pinning down. Or up.
Maybe it does. Maybe we all need either
a map or else, what is far worse, a net,
but matters are not so easily sorted,

a map can be a net, a net a map,

net map net map net map net map net map.

My friend Sabrina says I can sell a bridge.

She is a hematologist with Bayer,

lives in Atlanta with her husband, a chef.

She asked me to be VP of her foundation,

for anti-diabetes. You can sell

a bridge, she said. I looked at her and said,

I've sold the same bridge many, many times.

Is Brian O a bridge, a map, a net,

or all three things at once? Old woman sex.

I'm jetting between an old world and a new.

My friends are saying, Linda's got a boyfriend

in Europe, and you see things differently

when you hear someone talk about your life.

Just before lunch, I canceled my Ireland trip

and gave my eye surgery as an excuse,

and Brian texted back immediately,

when are you coming when the eye is done?

The fantasy must end. I'd rather it

happen by my own thought, by my own action.

I go to Ireland three times in a year;

I don't even go back to Singapore

once a year. My ex-father-in-law once

sent me a check to pay for my flight home,

and I used it to buy myself a car.

It's hard to let go. David T, my ex,

took seven years to agree to our divorce.

My mother said, if he loves you, he would

not let you go. My sister said my mom

would yell at David T for twenty minutes

before taking his money every week.

I said to my mom when I next saw her,

did you yell first or take the money first?

Where was I born? On Upper East Coast Road.

I remember going to the beach a lot.

Then our family moved to Opera Estate,

with roads named Tosca, Carmen, Aida,

ours the main road called Fidelio,

where we had a house, a car, and a garden,

and thought of ourselves as middle class.

Every morning the Indian gardener

fed the orchids cow dung and watered them.

It smelled when the sun rose. It did not smell

when it was dry. Now I can still smell it.

A Malay servant did the laundry. A

third servant did the shopping and the cooking.

I saw poor people first in their own homes

when I was training as a nurse in GH.

This old lady couldn't walk, so we went

to visit her in her house, really a hut,

the bed, bathroom, kitchen all in one space.

I was surprised you could do everything
in just one space. My closet at home was bigger.
I found married life boring—no need to clean,
no thought of volunteering, just mahjong
all day, every day, except church on Sunday.
When I complained to my mom, she forced me
to take up nursing, and, the irony,
nursing gave me a way to live away.
When I was first diagnosed in '94,
my first thought was how much easier would
life be in Singapore. I was scared shitless,
although I was not moaning about it.
From observation, there are just three kinds
of cancer patients. The kind that moans and groans.
The kind that bears it up stoically.
And the third kind, the kind that does not know
what they are feeling. I decided early
to be stoic was much more elegant.
To set my diamond in a two-prong setting.
How did I meet Brian O? On a cruise ship.
And then the postcards started to arrive.
My boyfriend then, Robert M, who's a Scot,
was playing with his band on board the ship
plowing the Caribbean. Sounds fun, right,
to be a part of a band's entourage?
It was not. Everyone was drinking themselves

silly. I was the only one not drinking.
The wives complaining that their husbands slept
all day and left the kids and chores to them.
Robert and I went camping in New England
with his two dogs. By 8 a.m., I was packed
and ready to leave, but he was still sleeping.
When I woke him up at ten, he snapped at me,
do you think life revolves around you?
I said, I waited for two freaking hours.
He went back to sleep, and I went back
to my apartment, changed my phone number,
unlisted it, and did not hear from him.
Robert M told his friends that I had left
because he didn't want to marry me.
I had not told him I was married still.
After leaving Singapore, I had no plans
to remarry soon. Robert used to say,
Linda P is my only girlfriend
who never clears my sink of dirty dishes.
It was half a complaint and half a boast.
I would say in reply, I did not come
to New York to wash anybody's dishes.
Always it was easier to say what I
did not come for than what I came for.
Life is a process of elimination,
said Linda P and cleaned her plate of cod.

We exist as long as somebody remembers us!

Five couples, ten of us, assembled by
Linda P for her dinner party, promised
more stories and insights into the hostess.
Remember, Linda P said. Don't tell them
you're writing about me, or else they won't
be honest. And I want them to be honest.
John R was honesty personified,
I thought, his figure tall and slightly bent
from years of helping patients breathe easier,
his face carved with a slightly startled look,
not for being caught in some secretive act,
but for thinking the world an honest place.
To questions about Croton and the dam,
he gave detailed replies, literal minded,
trustworthy as the houses that he built
each summer in New Orleans post-Katrina.
The dam was less impressive than I'd hoped,
showing it to my love, the architect,

the water level down, the river puling,

but he was taken with the structural feat,

the terraced wall, the patient, high-piled stone.

The Run for Hunger John R organized

each year raced over the long dam road,

and Daniel A, his cousin's husband, ran

once in the charity event. The judge

from California, the wife also a judge,

kept asking John to run in the Big Five,

a marathon in Africa so named

for the big animals of the safari.

You run past lions, prides of them, quite close,

Daniel said. They say it's all very safe.

After the pleasant detour to the dam,

soon we arrived at Linda and John's home,

John sliding the car right to the back door.

Linda has again outdone herself, Thea

announced as if the triumph was her own,

she has cooked up a storm. Turning to me,

she said, we're all dying to know how you

and Linda are related. Linda tells

such awful stories no one trusts her one bit.

A hint too bright, her voice was confident

it was the loveliest portion of the person

the clothes displayed to self-conscious effect.

My love took to her liveliness instantly.

She was the cousin, John's, from California,
tall, dark haired, full bosomed, a striking contrast
to Sophia, the psychologist, blond,
long as the stem of the wine glass she held
gracefully as she walked me to the couch.
She and her husband Drew, the neurosurgeon,
were the handsomest couple in the room,
he glowing with an aureole for hair
around a furrowed yet boyish brow.
Thea was right. Linda had cooked up a storm,
the dining table loaded like a boat
for Singapore, deep bowls of curry chicken,
lobster from Maine, fried bee hoon, Brussels sprouts.
It was to be an odyssey of eating,
and the test, not to be turned into pigs.
Mightier than the sorceress of the isle,
who knew of many drugs, Linda P knew
to make a conference of reasoning beasts.
Have you found out, demanded Linda P,
how Jee and I are related? He's your long-
lost brother, Thea said, found through FamilySearch.
Didn't your mother have a bastard son?
This from Vance, whom Linda kept calling Vince,
a barrel of a man and with a voice to match,
low, powerful, and tightly wound. Or else,
he said drily, your boy toy, as you said.

Vance's wife Joan threw a glance at my love
and looked down at her noodles tactfully.
Linda also said, interjected Sophia,
you're her therapist, in a tone that opened
the word to the widest interpretation.
Of a sort, I smiled. I just let her talk.
Thea was already off on another topic,
animatedly speaking of a case
that came before her bench the year before.
A child was sick, and both her parents, Christian
Scientists, basically asked the court
to rule against their religious beliefs
and order medical help for their child.
I mentioned Ian McEwan's *The Children Act*
and the dilemma suffered by the judge.
The court will always, Thea assured us all,
look out for the best interest of the child.
Linda looked thoughtful. Was she thinking of
Tatum and the highest court she knew,
Linda the girl-bride winning her reprieve,
her cancer-stamped career, her Brian O,
or just the curry chicken? No way to tell.
Even if there was a way, what would it say,
but it was what she thought in that split second?
Another second, and another thought,
the distant diamonds of the heaving sea.

Helping himself to more chicken, Vance,

whom Linda P kept calling Vince, with glee

informed the table that a rival researcher

was out to get him with a different theory.

The man was daily trolling him online,

and Vance was giving back good as he got.

My love, thinking to help with my research,

suggested that we each described our hostess

with just one word. And so we went around

the table with our succinct judgments. Thea:

Plucky. Vance: Headstrong. Sophia: Elegant.

John: Stubborn. My love: Creative. Joan: Proud. Drew:

Blunt. Daniel: Survivor. Me: Generous.

Every assessment also an assessment

of the assessor. How could it not be?

Thank you for your misjudgments, Linda said.

I thought you knew me well. Time for dessert,

John said and brought out not one but two pies,

a cherry and an apple pie, both looking

so good it was impossible to tell

which was shop-bought and which was made at home.

I've an announcement to make, John said,

after working for a good, long lifetime,

I'm retiring at the end of the year

and will have all the time to make more pies.

Glasses were raised, congratulations cheered,

the pies tasting as good as they appeared,

and so they disappeared. The women cleared

the table while the men tuned up their guitars.

First Vance sang to his and Drew's playing,

and combat in his voice yielded to a swoon.

I came in from the wilderness, Vance sang,

a creature void of form. Come on, she said,

I'll give ya shelter from the storm. My love

stopped talking to Joan about Tuscany

and told me with a hush it was Bob Dylan.

Then Drew's turn, and his pipes were silvery.

To taut and quivering strings, to Idiot Wind,

blowing like a circle around his skull,

from the Grand Coulee Dam to the Capitol,

he sang, you tame the lion in my cage.

When the men sang together the next song,

Vance taking the low road, and Drew the high,

they both admitted to their souls, you're a

big girl now. You're a big girl all the way.

The women joined in, claiming the accolade,

as Blood on the Tracks gave way to Desire,

but not before, certainly not before,

everyone sang of a simple twist of fate,

down by the docks, where sailors all come in.

11. Group email from Monkey, October 1, 2019

Books are mirrors: you only see in them what you already have inside
   of you!

12. Group email from Monkey, November 1, 2019

I am thankful for my struggles because without them I wouldn't have
   stumbled across my strength!

13. Group email from Monkey, December 1, 2019

You don't always have to tell people you love them.
You just have to give them no reason to doubt it.

14. Linda and John's house, Croton-on-Hudson, New York, February 1, 2020

New Year, the old replacement of what was
new, year of the white metal rat, plague year,
which would claim more than three million lives
around the world, the hospitals so stretched,
the old would be collected from the halls.
Mercifully ignorant, no bomoh
to tell Americans what was in store,
we met Rick and his fiancé Giovanni
at the train station, just as Linda wished,

and rode the iron horse along the river.
The boys were in love, hand searching for hand,
entangling, disentangling, and entangling
once more, resting at some points on the thigh.
We met in them the germ of our old passion
and smiled indulgently like second uncles,
or, rather, they indulged us with the treat
of youth and fervor and ideal ambition,
Rick affable as cookie dough ice cream
and Gio toothsome as pistachio gelato.
Linda P had prepared again a feast,
this time a Singaporean-styled steamboat,
king prawns, fillet of cod, beef, pork to cook
in a communal pot of chicken broth.
She had also prepared again a game,
another guessing game, teasing initials
printed by our names, all eight of them.
Catherine, whom Linda met at Woodbury Commons
twice on the same day and twice was mistaken
for Linda's daughter, though they looked so different,
was obvious. FD was, of course, Fake Daughter.
Eddie, her husband, hard because he had
no story told of him. Ricky was easy.
Hired by Linda at Sloan Kettering
for his first job, he was, in truth, Fake Son.
When he applied to nursing school, he wrote

the letter to be signed by Linda P,

who told him, Rick, you're good but not that good,

and had him change the recommendation

as a supportive but honest mother would.

He had just moved and would have Linda over

for dinner soon, but the apartment was

not ready to receive her in proper style.

At once I guessed IS, for me, stood for

Illegitimate Son, as Catherine did,

and so did Rick, and maybe you did too,

if you've been reading this with half a mind.

Fine word, illegitimate! So I played

the bastard uncle to my niece and nephew.

Linda was SAW, John RSH.

Dear Reader, can you guess what they stand for?

In the meantime, Rick and Giovanni talked

about their hunt for the right wedding venue,

a place both affordable and unique.

Immediately Linda knew just the place,

the Castle in Tarrytown, built by a playwright

and newspaper man, with majestic views

of the Hudson River and its various valleys,

the Oak Room trophied by the wainscoting

from the house Louis XIV gave James II,

when the emasculated king fled to France.

Rick laughed. It was so like Linda to give

such a preposterous idea. A castle!
My love suggested a converted barn
in Hudson, Catherine looked up some places,
and so the evening was merrily lost
to planning a grand fairy-tale wedding,
with flowers, diamond rings, and five-tiered cakes,
and family lost and found, and far and near.

15. Text Message, February 10, 2020

Today is difficult, Tatum's 10th anniversary.

16. My apartment, Marcus Garvey Park, Harlem, March 20, 2020

I don't usually dream, or rather I
don't usually remember any dream,
but last night I dreamed of Linda P,
and now I have the ending of this tale
of a Singaporean Wife of Bath.
In my dream, Linda P invited us
to a popiah lunch to celebrate
my turning fifty, and, sick of staying in,
we sailed once more to what we thought would be
a jaunt. About the house the hydrangeas
bloomed pink and blue and lavender, a sea,
as once she promised me. Sudden and swift

was the collapse, so compromised her body
—the wicked dream hastening the viral growth—
so sapped the walls holding the edifice.
John and the ventilator could not keep
her breathing, and she slipped into the breach,
after the rising numbers round the world.
Because of travel restrictions, only John
cried by her side, that afternoon, in Bethel,
a short six-minute walk from Asbury,
and then retired to his suffering.
Brian O would have flown there, but his sisters
restrained him, weeping for Linda and him.
Her comrades had their hands full of the virus.
In Bethel, she rested by her son, and I,
on scanning his obituary again,
his travels to the regions of the world,
Morocco, Ecuador, the Netherlands,
dreamed that he met her with his black sails,
cajoled her to join his voyage to Asia,
and she submitted to her wonder-boy,
on the condition that, on reaching Singapore,
he would lower the sails and raise the white,
so the authorities would let her in.
There she showed her son, walking to school,
two girls in Katong Convent uniform.
She and her older sister carried each

a pyramid of sugar for the bake sale
in aid of the association for the deaf,
except she had been pulling at a corner
and dripping sugar all the way from home,
a tiny trail of crystals, sharp as glass.
She cried because she now had nothing to offer,
and then her sister took her empty packet
from her mischievous hands and gave her hers.
I woke up at this point. It was my birthday.
I was fifty. The morning foggy first,
then sunny in the afternoon, then rainy.

OCCASIONAL POEMS

INFERIOR FURS

for Mark Yeo,

on appearing in "Gary Busey: Pet Judge"

For selling you a syndicate of inferior furs,
South African meerkats, you take to court
a man in a neck brace, cushioned support
for driving up in an SUV wheelchair.
Of course, the setup is a metaphor:
fragility—white fragility—for sport
is put on trial by some Asian passport,
cruelty to animals, and love of lucre.

Still, like the star turns of Anna May Wong,
you flaunt your IKEA curtain suit, hateful
with eyes—openly evil—on the con,
comical as the Black bailiff's one-liners,
and, for destroying your handbag career,
eyes on the judge who fractured, once, his skull.

GETTING HITCHED
ON ZOOM

for Tomson and Ruth,
September 12, 2020

Take one. Take two. Take them, or not.
They're here, and they're heirs of our broken spring and sick summer.

Future wives are about to show themselves, show you.
Get ready for small arts, puppets and bread.

The stags are out, and they mean business,
black and blue.

I'm organizing a rap video,
and you must come dressed in conceptual poetry.

The bike twerks down the Terengganu dirt track. The dirt track,
like a carpet, unrolls in Changi Airport.

Unless you hustle the cube of chicken stock in,
you won't husband soup.

Please ventilate what Gig Ryan, the Oz poet
with the non-binary name, calls "the unconditional rooms."

Nothing prepared us for the sky livestreaming like Facebook
and smelling like flowers.

The city maxed out its credit. Forgive the damage in advance.
They go we and not we, and us. They do.

ON GRADUATING FROM YOUR PLAYWRITING PROGRAM

for Zizi Azah

The times, they are against you, the *Times* too.
The chummy virus has closed down the lights,
for how long not one prophet can be sure,
and afterwards, if afterwards has rights,
the patient is unhooked from machine lungs,
totters, collapses here and there, eyes whites,
a modern Zinira whose mother tongues
holler unheard. Distant are the satellites.

Writing for TV is an option close
to blasphemy, betrayal, or bad works,
much as one loves the silver cellulose,
much as one envies its heroes and its jerks.
But live theater is bang on the nose,
not the image of faith but faith itself,

precise and literal and malodorous,

transforming us into a commonwealth.

We need plays! We need playwrights! The old term

recalling still of mills, wheels, ships, and carts.

Although the wilderness glares and grunts, be firm!

Glare back until the One who sees our hearts

brings to your side the tiger and the tick,

turning all counters into counterparts.

Grunt if you must, because the work is sick,

but Prophet you're, and Mistress of the Arts.

TERIMA KASIH

for Eli Tyler,

for his show at the New York Botanical Garden, April 2019

Tune in to Eli, tune in, tune into
Mouli's kite flying in a loop of song,
a lash of night jasmine, Teresa sweet,
into Turavi's wooden boat, afloat
the sampan looking for the fisherman
(the beach is blue), tune in thank you, thank you,
for big Mustafa's turtle cape, ninja
ready, say again terima kasih,
because Singa the lion's chilly breath
can rip the skin off your ass, because
the bamboo dies to become the angklung,
klung, klung, tune in to Teochew opera
and sample the queer cymbals, whistles, drums,
on Nek Nek's surprise visit one night
to blow out Siti's Deepavali lights.
Oh, Sayang's local train, the long procession
of accents, dictions, dialects, rhetorics,

the true and the false etymologies,

sample and loop, live sample and live loop,

for a living technique against the ear.

In Ekkam's garden home, the children sing,

Eli sings, gelang sipaku gelang,

and homewards with the iron orchids goes

the only lily in the orchid show.

ACKNOWLEDGMENTS

My heartfelt gratitude to all the Singaporeans who told me their stories and gave me permission to write and publish them. Thank you for your trust. I believe our stories form one vital strand in the rope of Singapore history. And not just Singapore, but also the history of the United States of America.

I am grateful to the editors of the following publications for first publishing poems in this book:

Blackbox Manifold, Borderless Journal, Creative Flight, Eunoia Review, Impossible Archetype, Jogos Florais, Mānoa, Mekong Review, Mollyhouse, Poetry London, Quarterly Literary Review of Singapore, this/that/lit, Vice-Versa.

Big thanks to my editor, Kimberley Lim, for her meticulous and miraculous attention.

Always, my love to my love, Guy E. Humphrey. For loving this Singaporean in America.

ABOUT THE AUTHOR

Jee Leong Koh is a Singaporean writer, editor, and publisher living in New York City. His hybrid work *Snow at 5 PM: Translations of an Insignificant Japanese Poet* won the 2022 Singapore Literature Prize in English fiction. His book of poems *Steep Tea* (Carcanet) was named a Best Book of the Year by the *Financial Times* in the UK and a finalist by Lambda Literary in the US. Other honors include being shortlisted twice for the Singapore Literature Prize in English poetry for *The Pillow Book* and *Connor & Seal*. His book reviews have appeared in the *TLS*, *PN Review*, and elsewhere.

From the Latin *gaudium,* meaning "joy," Gaudy Boy publishes books that delight readers with the various powers of art. The name is taken from the poem "Gaudy Turnout," by Singaporean poet Arthur Yap, about his time abroad in Leeds, the United Kingdom. Similarly inspired by such diasporic wanderings and migrations, Gaudy Boy brings literary works by authors of Asian heritage to the attention of an American audience and beyond. Established in 2018 as the imprint of the New York City-based literary nonprofit Singapore Unbound, we publish poetry, fiction, and literary nonfiction.

Visit our website at www.singaporeunbound.org/gaudyboy.

Winners of the Gaudy Boy Poetry Book Prize

Waking Up to the Pattern Left By a Snail Overnight
by Jim Pascual Agustin

Time Regime
by Jhani Randhawa

Object Permanence
by Nica Bengzon

Play for Time
by Paula Mendoza

Autobiography of Horse
by Jenifer Sang Eun Park

The Experiment of the Tropics
by Lawrence Lacambra Ypil

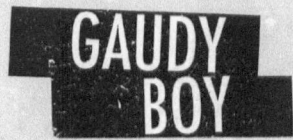

Fiction and Nonfiction

Lovelier, Lonelier
by Daryl Qilin Yam

Bengal Hound
by Rahad Abir

The Infinite Library and Other Stories
by Victor Fernando R. Ocampo

The Sweetest Fruits
by Monique Truong

And the Walls Come Crumbling Down
by Tania De Rozario

The Foley Artist
by Ricco Villanueva Siasoco

Malay Sketches
by Alfian Sa'at

Other Series

New Singapore Poetries
edited by Marylyn Tan and Jee Leong Koh

Suspect: Volume 1, Year 1
edited by Jee Leong Koh

From Gaudy Boy Translates

Picking off new shoots will not stop the spring
edited by Ko Ko Thett and Brian Haman

Amanat
edited by Zaure Batayeva and Shelley Fairweather-Vega

Ulirát
edited by Tilde Acuña, John Bengan, Daryll Delgado, Amado Anthony G.
Mendoza III, and Kristine Ong Muslim

Books by our other imprint, Bench Press

Snow at 5 PM: Translations of an Insignificant Japanese Poet
by Jee Leong Koh

Seven Studies for a Self-Portrait: Poems
by Jee Leong Koh

Equal to the Earth: Poems
by Jee Leong Koh

Lightly in the Good of Day
by Bob Hart

Try to Have Your Writing Make Sense:
The Quintessential PFFA Anthology: Poems
edited by Donna Smith and Howard Miller